T0341631

Nothing
But the Truth

John Kani

WITWATERSRAND UNIVERSITY PRESS

Witwatersrand University Press
1 Jan Smuts Avenue
Johannesburg
2001
South Africa

First published 2002
Reprinted in 2004, 2007, 2009, 2010, 2011, 2012, 2013, 2014, 2015, 2016 and 2017

ISBN 978-1-86814-389-4

Cover photograph: 'You burnt my brother'

Photographs by Ruphin Coudyzer
Cover Design and Typesetting by Crazy Cat Designs,
Johannesburg, South Africa
Printed and bound by Creda Communications

Dedicated to my brother,
Xolile Kani.

Introduction

Zakes Mda

The world premier of *Nothing But the Truth* at the National Festival of the Arts in Grahamstown was hailed by critics variously as one of the greatest days in South African theatre history and a pivotal cultural moment. Alan Swerdlow commented that Kani had written a play that was so brimming with humanity and compassion, married seamlessly with its intellectual standpoint, that the audience left the theatre elated and stimulated. In the same article, Darryl Accone pointed out that this was indeed the play the new South Africa had been waiting for. It dealt with the contradictions of liberation and the perplexities of freedom in an utterly exhilarating manner. He added, 'Strikingly, beneath its humour and humanity, *Nothing But the Truth* is a deeply political play of immense subtlety and depth.'[1] Another critic, Guy Willoughby, trumpeted that the thematic terrain explored was fascinating, taking South Africa out of the didactic 'protest' stage mode into theatrical forms that conveyed the complex political dynamics of the democratic era.[2] The audiences agreed. The full-house performances received standing ovations.

This turning point in South African drama began with a casual conversation outside a restaurant in the Market Theatre precinct. I mentioned to John Kani that I was bothered by the references that were often made to *Sizwe Bansi is Dead* and *The Island* as Athol Fugard's plays, without ever crediting John Kani and Winston Ntshona. This is common not only in the academy but also among international theatre practitioners and commentators. Some are indeed generous enough to mention Kani and Winston Ntshona, but reduce them to Fugard's appendages who happened to be present when the great master wrote the two plays. Yet these plays are a result of the creative synergy of three great creators: Fugard, Kani and Ntshona, in an alphabetic order that has unfortunately conferred on the first name the status of the sole or — at the very least — supreme creator. I know from my association with some of the artists of the Serpent Players — the New Brighton, Port Elizabeth, theatre company to which the creators of the seminal works belonged — that without Kani and Ntshona *Sizwe Bansi is Dead* and *The Island* would never have been written. These plays tell the stories of New Brighton, and of black South Africa from an insider's perspective and are indeed informed by the experiences of the two co-creators, their friends and their relatives.

Even as I expressed my indignation Kani did not seem overly concerned with being marginalised from his own creations. He knew the role he had played in the writing of these South African modern classics and that was enough for him. It was not enough for me. I thought it was important to set the record straight for posterity. But then there was a nagging question that needed to be answered: if theatre commentators like me insist that Kani played such a pivotal role in creating these plays why has he never written a play since? Why did his playwriting flair disappear with the departure of Athol Fugard from their common New Brighton hub of creativity? I had been asked this question before, and had only managed to tender the flimsy excuse that the man was busy focusing on his work as an actor, as the managing trustee of the Market Theatre, the chairman of the National Arts Council and a social activist who sits on the boards of many organisations.

'As long as you have not written a single play since the days of your association with Athol Fugard, people will continue to ask me this irritating question,' I told him, 'You must empower me with an answer.'

He responded: 'There is this play that I have always wanted to write, but never found the time to get down to it.'

Then he told me the fascinating story of the two brothers, of sibling rivalry, of exile, of memory and identity, of reconciliation and justice! Above all, it was a human story full of compassion. The very compassion and humanity that was later identified by the critics. And we all know that it is compassion, humanity and tolerance that distinguish great art from mediocre. I knew at once we had the makings of a great play and I was going to hound him until he wrote it. And I did.

I was not in the least surprised that there was this great play residing so comfortably in the recesses of Kani's imagination. A man of such presence and humour, a man who can cook up a powerful impromptu speech at the drop of a hat, a natural storyteller, a man of such profound insights, a Tony award-winning actor … there must be a play in him! There must be many plays in him!

After all, Kani comes from a long tradition of creating plays, and not just of interpreting other people's work as an actor and later director. *Nothing But the Truth* may be his debut as a solo playwright, but he has been involved in creating plays since the day he joined the Serpent Players in 1965 and came into contact with Athol Fugard, Winston Ntshona and other theatre practitioners such as Nomhle Nkonyeni and Fats Bookholane, who later distinguished themselves on the South African and international stage and screen. Before the two best-known works, *Sizwe Bansi* (1972) and *The Island*

(1973), there was *The Coat* in 1965[3], and then a series of plays that were jointly created and performed to a resounding reception but were never published. These include *The Last Bus* (1966), dealing with relationships between the African and coloured people of Port Elizabeth, *Friday's Bread on Monday* (1967), which addressed poverty; a satirical look at black-on-black exploitation titled *The Cure* and adapted from Machiavelli's *The Mandrake* in 1968, and *The Sell Out*, on police informers in 1971.

Nothing But the Truth belongs to a body of post-apartheid work that has been referred to as 'Theatre for Reconciliation'. However, it exposes the shortcomings of reconciliation as espoused by our political leaders, who focused on reconciliation between blacks and whites, and forgot that there is a dire need for reconciliation among the blacks themselves. The play also illustrates quite vividly why it is still necessary to talk about the past: because the past will always be a powerful presence in the present.

The play validates what I have written elsewhere about how vital memory is to identity. Memory loss leads to loss of identity, because who we are is fundamentally linked to memory.

I have stated that there is an attempt in some sectors of South Africa to erase the past in order to reconstruct a new collective identity that will transform race and ethnic bound identities to a new South African national identity. In my view this is not a laudable development. The beauty of South Africa lies in its many cultures, each with its own history. Then there is of course, our collective history, emanating from the interactions of those cultures. The memory of each peculiar past can only enrich our present.

There is a demand from some of my compatriots that, since we have now attained democracy, we should all have collective amnesia, because memory does not contribute to reconciliation. Our new identity-in-the-making is threatened by memory. We should, therefore, not only forgive the past, we should also forget it. However, it is impossible to meet this demand, for we are products of our past. We have been shaped by our history. Our present worldview and our mindset is a result of our yesterdays.

If South Africa is to survive and prosper reconciliation is absolutely essential. But true reconciliation will only happen when we are able to confront what happened yesterday without bitterness. We cannot just sweep it under the carpet and hope that suddenly we will live in brotherly and sisterly love in a state of blissful amnesia.

For those of us who are survivors of the past it is important that we do not forget. We owe it to future generations that what happened to us must never happen again. It must never be repeated by those who oppressed us before. But most importantly, we ourselves must never assume the new role of oppressor. And only history can teach us those lessons.

We must never forget, but this does not mean we must cling to the past, and wrap it around us, and live for it, and be perpetual victims wallowing in masochistic memory of our national humiliation. We only look back to the past in order to have a better understanding of our present. This is one of the greatest lessons of *Nothing But the Truth*.

1 Accone, D. 'The Trouble with Freedom.' *Cue* 5 July 2002.

2 Willoughby, G. 'Theatre Pick of theWeek'. *Mail & Guardian* 19-25 July 2002.

3 Published in *My Children! My Africa! and selected shorter plays*. Witwatersrand University Press 1990.

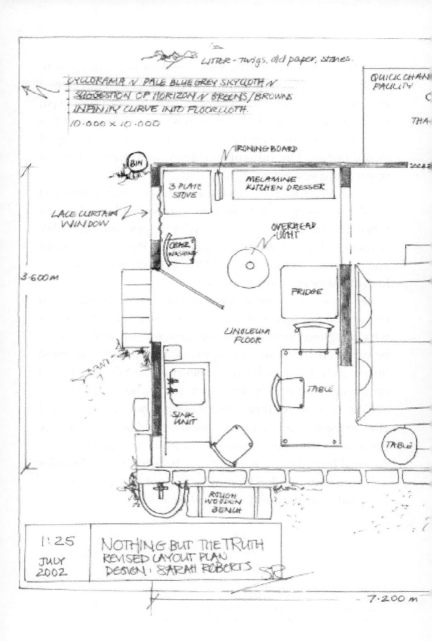

LITTER - Twigs, old paper, stones.

CYCLORAMA ~ PALE BLUE GREY SKYCLOTH ~
SUGGESTION OF HORIZON ~ GREENS/BROWNS
INFINITY CURVE INTO FLOORCLOTH.
10.000 × 10.000

QUICK CHAN
FACILITY

THA-

IRONING BOARD

BIN

3 PLATE
STOVE

MELAMINE
KITCHEN DRESSER

LACE CURTAIN
WINDOW

CHAIR
WASHING

OVERHEAD
LIGHT

3.600 M

FRIDGE

LINOLEUM
FLOOR

TABLE

SINK
UNIT

TABLE

ROUGH
WOODEN
BENCH

1:25
JULY
2002

NOTHING BUT THE TRUTH
REVISED LAYOUT PLAN
DESIGN : SARAH ROBERTS

7.200 M

x

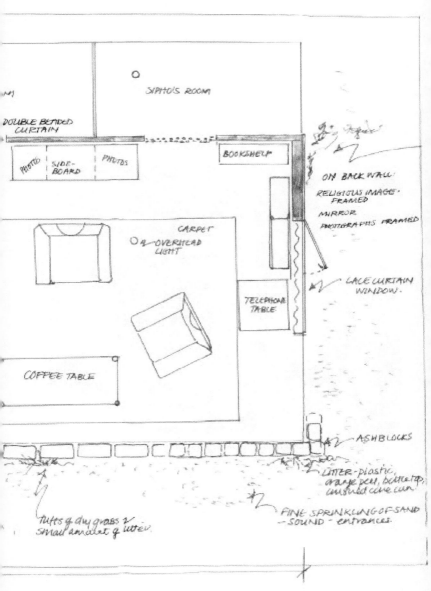

Sarah Roberts's design for the set of Nothing But the Truth

The living room of the Makhaya's New Brighton home

Cast

SIPHO MAKHAYA ... Assistant Chief Librarian at the Port Elizabeth Public Library where he has worked for almost 33 years.

THANDO MAKHAYA ... his only daughter, a teacher, who also works as an interpreter at the Amnesty hearings of the Truth and Reconciliation Commission.

MANDISA MACKAY... his English-born niece.

Nothing But The Truth premièred at the National Festival of the Arts in Grahamstown on 4 July 2002. The production was directed by Janice Honeyman, with set and costume design by Sarah Roberts and lighting design by Mannie Manim. The production was stage managed by Lebogang Mnisi.

Sipho was played by John Kani, Thando by Dambisa Kente and Mandisa by Pamela Nomvete.

The play was subsequently performed with the same cast at the Baxter Theatre, Cape Town, in July 2002, and at The Market Theatre, Johannesburg, in September 2002 with Nthati Moshesh in the role of Thando.

Act 1

A simple four-roomed house in New Brighton, Port Elizabeth. Built in the 1960s, the house is constructed of grey ash blocks or wind bricks. It comprises a front living area, divided into kitchen and living room by means of a partition, and two bedrooms accessed via the living room. Both kitchen and living room open into the yard. The space is small and cramped, the stage house, 7.2 metres wide by 3.6 metres deep, closely approximates to the actual size of a township dwelling. The living room is simply furnished, reflecting the modest means of a family of average income. The audience does not see the two bedrooms, the characters constantly move through the bead curtains into these private domains, and conversations continue through the walls, as they would in any domestic situation. There is no bathroom in the house — and the implication is that the toilet is located outside.

Scene 1

It is Thursday evening. SIPHO *is dressing up. He boils water on the stove, saving some for* THANDO.

SIPHO: Typical. Just like him. Always not there to take responsibility. Even when we were kids. It was never his fault. Even when he lost my blazer, it wasn't his fault. So said my Mother. Damn you Themba. All I wanted was a little time. Just for the two of us. There are things I wanted to talk to you about. There are questions I needed to ask. But no. Themba doesn't arrive. He is not available. As

2

usual. I am the eldest. I must understand. [*Checks the time.*] Oh my God. Where is Thando? It's getting late. [*Goes to the telephone and dials.*] Hello, is that Mr. Khahla — it's me, yes Sipho. No, not yet. I was just reminding you. [THANDO *rushes in, carrying her briefcase, handbag and books.*] Yes, we will be ready. OK Mr. Khahla ...

THANDO: I am home. I am sorry I'm late.

SIPHO: Shh! No, No, it's still OK. I've just called the undertaker. Any way we still have time. There is hot water for you in the kettle if you want to freshen up.

THANDO: Oh Daddy you really spoil me, you know. Thanks. Hey, any news about the job?

She goes into her room.

SIPHO: Nothing yet. We are still waiting but my second interview went well today. He was very impressed. He said I knew everything. I could even manage the library on my own. The only concern was my age. But it didn't really matter, he said.

THANDO [*back in the living room*]: Were they the same people who interviewed you the last time?

SIPHO: No. It was just the Chief Director of Language and Heritage. He said even Mrs. Potgieter recommended me strongly.

THANDO: Mrs. Potgieter, is she still there?

SIPHO: Yes. But she has made it clear that she will not be available to continue after the restructuring. She is applying for an early retirement package. She says it's time a black person took over. She says the library will be in good hands with me in charge.

THANDO: And so ...

SIPHO: Look, I've got about two years to go before I retire. But it would be nice if it happens.

THANDO: Aren't you nervous?

SIPHO: About the job?

THANDO: No. About this evening?

SIPHO: No. I am just not sure about the procedure. I have his old passbook but I could not find his birth certificate. This baptismal certificate is all I have.

THANDO: A baptismal certificate, of course, that's all you old people have. The only proof for black people that they truly existed [*laughs*].

SIPHO: I've never been comfortable seeing dead people. Even family. My father had to push me forward to see my mother just before they closed the coffin. I don't want that image to be the last thing I remember about a person. Also I was a bit afraid.

THANDO: Afraid?

SIPHO: No. Themba was different, though.

THANDO: You mean more brave?

SIPHO: I said different! ... and now I have to collect his body from the airport. I don't know what he looks like now, I haven't seen him for over twenty years.

THANDO: People don't change. Not that much.

SIPHO: No. Not Themba. He would never change.

THANDO: I really wanted to meet Uncle Themba. Everybody said so much about him. Was he handsome?

SIPHO: Why?

THANDO: All the ladies in our township say so. Everyone keeps saying "Oh, that was a man!"

SIPHO: Yeah, he was a bit of a lady's man.

THANDO: And a comrade ... I mean a man of the Struggle.

SIPHO [*withdrawing into himself*]: Yes, he was.

THANDO: Come on Tata. Tell me more about him.

SIPHO: The undertaker is going to be here any moment now. I do not want to make him wait.

4

THANDO: It's funny, every time I try to make you talk about Uncle Themba you change the subject. All I know about him is what everybody else has told me.

SIPHO: I've told you everything there is to know.

THANDO: Were you close?

SIPHO: With whom?

THANDO: Uncle Themba.

SIPHO: He is dead.

THANDO: I mean before, before he left.

SIPHO: He is my brother

THANDO: He must have been very close to Grandpa. Uncle Themba, that's all he talked about.

SIPHO: Of course my father always talked about Themba. When Themba left the country, at first my father blamed me for not stopping him.

THANDO: Really? I never knew that Grandpa felt that way. To me he said he loved you very much.

SIPHO: I wish he had told me too.

THANDO: You mean Grandpa never said he loved you?

SIPHO: We African men don't find it easy to say that to our sons. It's taken for granted that we do.

THANDO: Was Uncle Themba close to Mom?

SIPHO: What do you mean?

THANDO: People say they got along very well.

SIPHO: Who are these people saying these things to you?

THANDO: Well everybody …

SIPHO: I suppose they were close, very close. He was my brother.

THANDO: Why did Uncle Themba go into exile?

SIPHO: HE LEFT THE COUNTRY! Leave it at that. [*Pause.*] Why are you asking these questions?

THANDO: Mandisa will be here any time now. I know nothing about her father. What am I going to talk about?

5

What is she going to think of me when I tell her that I don't know her father? [*Pause.*] People say he was a political activist. Weren't you proud of him? I would be.

SIPHO: Oh yes, he was an activist. Believe me he was an activist. He caused a lot of trouble for everyone and a lot more for himself

THANDO: And Luvuyo? People talk about him too. Especially the young people. Sometimes I wish he was alive. It would have been nice to have a brother. Someone to be there for you.

SIPHO: And me? Am I not here for you?

THANDO: Of course, you are always here for me. A brother would have been different. I understand he too was close to Uncle Themba.

SIPHO: Everybody was close to Themba.

THANDO: You must miss him a lot.

SIPHO: Themba?

THANDO: Luvuyo.

SIPHO: Yes I do.

THANDO: And Uncle Themba?

SIPHO: How was your day?

THANDO: Oh! The same grind. Former soldiers, policemen and security people applying for amnesty. Saying they are sorry. Sometimes I sit there translating, interpreting, and not even feeling. Its easy to get numb you know.

SIPHO: That's why I do not go anymore. It's pointless.

THANDO: The truth does come out, and at least the families get to know what happened.

SIPHO: Their version of what happened.

THANDO: Don't start! Don't start! I know how you feel about that.

Pause.

SIPHO: The undertaker must be on his way now.

THANDO [*as she exits*]: Daddy, what did Uncle Themba die of?

SIPHO: His heart gave in, so says his wife.

THANDO [*from the bedroom*]: Why didn't Auntie Thelma accompany his body instead of Mandisa?

SIPHO: The letter just said 'My daughter will be coming with him'. He wanted to be buried here at home, not far from Mom and Dad.

THANDO: Why didn't Uncle Themba come back when most of the exiles came home?

SIPHO: They were settled and comfortable where they were. Many exiles felt that way. Some came back to look around, to check out the scene, so to speak. Then realised that they would be better off where they had jobs, families.

THANDO: But Bra Hugh, Sis Miriam and the others, they came back.

SIPHO: That's different. Some had homes and families to come home to. Some had jobs in the government.

THANDO: So why did Uncle Themba not even visit after the first election! He could have? Couldn't he?

SIPHO [*after a long pause*]: HE DIDN'T! Is the Cradock case over?

THANDO [*coming back into the room*]: Tomorrow.

SIPHO: You think they are going to get amnesty?

THANDO: I don't know. I am not the judge.

SIPHO: Is everything OK?

THANDO: Yes! Why?

SIPHO: Because you always know.

THANDO: One gets confused sometimes. Especially when so many lies are told. One loses perspective. You find yourself wanting to believe. I don't know why I am doing this because it's not for the money.

SIPHO: You can stop anytime you want. Where is Mr Khahla? I want to be there when the plane arrives.

THANDO [*looking at her watch*]: We still have time. I wonder what she looks like?

SIPHO: Who?

THANDO: My sister, Mandisa.

SIPHO: If she is Themba's daughter, I will know her.

THANDO: I bet she looks like Uncle Themba.

SIPHO: She could also look like her mother.

THANDO [*laughing*]: And me?

SIPHO: I have told you already. You look like your mother.

Long pause.

THANDO: Oh yes. My mother … There's another mystery. Not a word, not even a letter from her. All I have is that picture of both of you in front of the library in town. Nothing else. You think she's still alive?

SIPHO: Who?

THANDO: My mother.

SIPHO: Yes.

THANDO: Have you tried to find her?

SIPHO: She left me. I don't think she wanted to be found.

THANDO: And me?

SIPHO: No. She loved you very much.

THANDO: How can you say that! How could you know that?

SIPHO: I know. She loved you.

THANDO: How could you know that!

SIPHO: Because I do!

THANDO: There are three things you know because you do. Three things you do not want to talk about — my mother, my brother, Luvuyo, and my Uncle Themba.

SIPHO: Let the dead rest.

THANDO: You have just said my mother is not dead.

SIPHO: I know.

THANDO: Because you do.

SIPHO: Are we going to use your car to follow the undertaker. I don't fancy riding in the hearse.

THANDO: Of course. You are alive aren't you? How could I let you ride in a hearse?

SIPHO: Not yet. It's not my time yet. This old ticker [*pointing to his heart*] tells me it's not going to be long though.

THANDO: You! You will outlive us all.

SIPHO: That's what my father said. It's like a punishment, to witness the pain of losing all those you love, to be alone.

THANDO: Dad, you will never be alone. I'll always be with you.

SIPHO: What about Mpho! When you get married?

THANDO: Oh yes, that's another one you never talk about. I am surprised you have actually mentioned his name. Anyway he knows it's the full package. You and me or nothing.

SIPHO: No, Thando, no package. It's you only. We should go now.

THANDO: Now that you have mentioned it Mpho's uncles want to come and discuss lobola with you.

SIPHO: After the funeral.

THANDO: Let me fix your tie.

SIPHO: I am nervous.

THANDO: What, to meet Uncle Themba? He's dead. He won't know how you look.

SIPHO: No, it's Mandisa.

THANDO: You want to look good for her.

SIPHO: She's from England.

THANDO: So?

SIPHO: I don't know what her father has told them about me, about us.

THANDO: Whatever it is, we are about to find out, aren't we

SIPHO: Still, do I look OK?

THANDO: Daddy, you've got your Sunday suit on. You look good. Just like you've always looked. My Dad. That's enough for me. It's going to have to do for her too and everybody else.

SIPHO: It's twenty-five years. He was standing right where you are standing, next to the door. Turned around and walked away. I've had so many dreams about him. He is always coming towards me and just as I am about to talk to him or call his name, I always wake up. In all those dreams I could never see his face clearly. Is his hair grey now? It's strange. This is not the way I've always imagined our meeting.

Silence.

THANDO: What now? What are you thinking about?

SIPHO: When I was a little boy I made myself a wire double decker bus. I spent four days non-stop at it. When it was finished I drove it around for about three minutes and Themba wanted it for himself. He cried. My father shouted at me: 'What's the matter with you? Give it to him. Can't you see he is crying?' I gave it to him. He wrenched it out of my hands. My finger bled a little, because of the force with which he grabbed it from me. The wire cut my finger. He drove it away. I watched him go with a piece of my heart and love for my wire bus. Themba had a lot of toy cars my father bought for him from town. He did not need that wire bus. He took it because it was mine.

THANDO: What happened to the car — the wire bus?

10

SIPHO: It lasted for a day or two. The last time I saw it, it was smashed. Themba was driving it on the street, a bakery van surprised him, he ran off, leaving my bus on the road, the van smashed it flat. I was so angry. I wanted to kill him. My mother got angry with me. 'It was nothing. Just a bus made of wire.' Funny, I've never forgotten that wire bus. I can still see it, very clearly, in my mind. Will he be in one of those black body bags?

THANDO: No, that's only in the movies. He will be in a coffin.

SIPHO: Yes, you are right. Are you sure, we've got everything?

THANDO: I am sure Mandisa has all the documents. All you have to do is to identify the body. The undertaker is also with us; he will know what to do. [*Sound of a car hooter.*] You have bought the ox as well to be slaughtered at the funeral?

SIPHO: Oh my God, I never asked him to bring an empty coffin with him. To put Themba's body in.

THANDO: Will you stop worrying. I told you he will be in a coffin. The undertaker knows these things. Come on!

She exits.

SIPHO: Now I am really nervous.

He exits.

'What is in this thing?' Pamela Nomvete (Mandisa) and
John Kani (Sipho)

12

Scene 2

The same house. The lights come up slowly on the empty living room. SIPHO *comes in carrying an urn. He puts it down on the coffee table and sits down on his chair, eyes fixed on the urn.* THANDO *enters, carrying as many suitcases and bags as she can, followed by* MANDISA, *about 22 years old, well dressed, beautiful and glamorous, as one would expect from someone who grew up in London. She is carrying a fashion designer's portfolio and a bag from an airport duty free shop.*

THANDO: Put everything down here now.

MANDISA: Are you sure, Thando? I did book myself into the Garden Court Plaza Hotel.

THANDO: No! You are going to stay here with us. My father insists. Yes, Daddy. You have to be here until the funeral on Saturday.

SIPHO: The funeral! Oh, my God! The funeral! What are we going to do? What about the night vigil? Reverend Haya is coming soon to conduct a small service for the arrival of Themba's body. What body? How could you do this to me? Why didn't your mother say anything to me?

MANDISA: My mother wrote to you, Uncle Sipho, and you never replied. Anyway, I don't see the problem. That's what everybody does in England.

SIPHO: You burnt my brother.

MANDISA: Don't say burnt. He was cremated, and that was my mother's wish.

SIPHO: Your mother's wish. You burnt him to ashes.

THANDO: Daddy, please!

SIPHO [*pointing to the urn*]: What is in this thing?

13

MANDISA: His ashes.

SIPHO: All of him?

MANDISA: Some of him.

SIPHO: Where is the rest?

MANDISA: You don't take all the ashes from the oven. It's symbolic. The rest is … discharged is the word they use.

SIPHO: You mean thrown away?

MANDISA: All right. Yes.

SIPHO: I want them all.

MANDISA: Oh this is ridiculous. I didn't come here to argue about ashes.

SIPHO: What am I going to bury on Saturday? My uncles are going to want to see him. What is going to be in the coffin?

THANDO: Daddy! Some black people here are also going in for cremation these days.

SIPHO: I am not some black people. I am me. My family does not do that. The letter said 'Mandisa will be coming with him'.

MANDISA: I did. I brought his ashes.

SIPHO [*showing a letter*]: This letter said Mandisa would be coming with my brother. That is why I arranged a funeral. I could have organised a memorial in the St Stephen's Church Hall. He wanted to be buried next to my Mom and Dad, said the letter. No one said he wants his ashes to be scattered beside his Mom and Dad's grave. You have embarrassed me. Hurt me. She should have asked me whether the family objected to my brother being cremated. No one asked me. I am his brother. I am his family.

THANDO: Let's all be calm and discuss this.

SIPHO: Oh my God! The undertaker! Did you pay him Thando?

THANDO: Yes I did.

14

SIPHO: What did he say?

THANDO: I've never seen Mr Khahla so confused. He said he would talk to you later about the funeral arrangements, if any.

SIPHO: I must go and talk to him and Reverend Haya and my Uncle to sort this out.

He rushes out.

MANDISA: Bloody Hell! That was some welcome!

THANDO: Please understand that the whole thing took my father by surprise. He never expected this [*pointing to the urn*]. He's talked about nothing these past days but his brother's funeral. He will be OK once he has spoken to his uncle and Reverend Haya. He is happy to see you here. That's why you must stay here with us until you go back to London. I know that is what he wants also. Please stay.

MANDISA: All right, I will stay here if it's OK with you.

THANDO: It is OK with both my father and me. That's what your father would have wanted.

MANDISA: Can I use the phone to call the Garden Court Plaza and cancel my reservation?

THANDO: There it is … in the corner there.

She starts taking the suitcases into the other room.

MANDISA [*dialing*]: Everything was arranged by my travel agent. Mom and I did not anticipate an elaborate funeral … Hello … hello … My name is Ms Mandisa McKay … McKay … I have a reservation with you. UK … yes … I wish to cancel this reservation … yes, I know … that is unfortunate, I am going to stay with my family.

THANDO [*softly*]: My family!

MANDISA: Yes … yes. I am sorry if I have caused any inconvenience — thank you.

15

She puts down the telephone.

THANDO: Welcome home.

MANDISA: Home. That's all we talked about with my father. He's always said to me 'England is not your home, it's just where you live. It's where your house is. My home is in South Africa, 46 Madala Street, New Brighton, Port Elizabeth. That's where your home is, African Princess.'

THANDO: African Princess? That's what my father used to call me too when I was young.

MANDISA: It always made me feel so African.

THANDO: On the phone you said Ms McKay.

MANDISA: Yes, I know. It's Mandisa Makhaya. They decided to register me at birth as Mandisa McKay. I suppose it was to help us fit in. But I've always known that I am ... don't laugh ... I am going to try to say it like my father taught me: 'Ndiyintombi yakwa Makhaya ema Chireni'.

THANDO [*laughing*]: Ndiyintombi yakwa Makhaya e Ma Cireni.

MANDISA: I am happy to be home.

THANDO: I am happy too, my sister. With you I can at least introduce you to my friends as my sister. I've never had anyone my age that I am related to. It's always been ... 'Meet your uncle. Meet your aunt.' This is my dadobawo or this is your malume.

MANDISA: You are still better off than me. All I knew were children of my father's friends in exile. Only when we went to visit my mother's people in Barbados could I say that I was with family. But my father always said, 'These are your mother's people. Your family is in South Africa.' God, that used always to make my mother mad.

THANDO: Barbados?

MANDISA: In the West Indies. My mom was the second generation of her family born in London. She is still so proud of her West Indian roots.

THANDO: She must be beautiful. Your hair …

MANDISA: Yes. That's what I got from her, only the hair, as my father would tease me. He always said I looked like his Aunt Mandisa.

THANDO: Dadobawo Mandisa

MANDISA: Say that again

THANDO: Dadobawo Mandisa, our great aunt on my father's side.

Pause.

MANDISA: It's great to be here with you at last, my cousin Thando.

THANDO: Uh-Uh. My sister, Mandisa. Your father and my father were brothers. In my family that makes us sisters.

MANDISA: What's a cousin then?

THANDO: If you were my father's sister's child, then you would be my cousin, as we would not share the same clan and surname.

MANDISA: So you are my sister?

THANDO: Yes I am, yes I am …

Look at me, where is my hospitality! [*She takes the remaining suitcase and the duty free bag into her bedroom.*] Let me help you put these bags in my room. There are two beds in there. 'Just in case'… as my father always says. I'm glad. We've got so much to talk about.

MANDISA: This is just as my father described.

THANDO: What?

MANDISA: This house. Everything … the bookshelves, pictures on the wall, even the smell. Everything.

THANDO [*coming out of the bedroom and going into the kitchen to make a salad*]: What smell?

MANDISA: The township smell — the dust, coal stoves ... something earthy, nothing like England or London especially.

THANDO: What does London smell like?

MANDISA: I never thought about it. My father always told me about the good smell of the township. The smell of the people — houses, dogs, rubbish, unkempt gardens, shebeens, skokiaan joints, all put together making the smell of life.

THANDO : He sure had the gift of the gab — that's Uncle Themba. [*She finishes the salad.*] Everybody remembers him for that. Bring the tray. Tell me about your father and your mother and you, of course.

MANDISA: Who first? Well I was born in Camden Town, a kind of a middle-class London suburb and went to the best schools, of course. Father wanted me to study medicine — 'There is a shortage of doctors at home'. He always reminded us of the needs of 'home', South Africa. But I went to college and studied fashion design.

That is why I have to be back in London by Monday or Tuesday by the latest as the London fashion shows start soon. I've brought some of my designs hoping to show them to some people in the business. I've always felt that my designs could use some African influence.

She puts the portfolio on the coffee table.

THANDO [*looking at some of Mandisa's sketches*]: I know of someone who could be of great help to you in that regard, but she lives in Johannesburg. Her name is Nandipa Madikiza. She's the best in this country.

18

MANDISA: Yeah, I've heard about her. You must introduce me to her please!

THANDO: I don't know her personally. I know of her work. But you say you have to leave by Tuesday?

MANDISA: Yes. Why don't you come with me to Johannesburg to meet her?

THANDO: You are not staying a little longer ... I mean to mourn?

MANDISA: My father died two weeks ago. I've done all the mourning ... I've got work to do now.

THANDO: My father would expect us to show some respect for at least a month as children. Elderly people mourn much longer. He won't allow me to go with you to Jo'burg.

MANDISA: Girl! 'He won't allow you'!

THANDO: Things are different here. This is not London. There are rules in this house. For as long as I am staying with him under his roof there are rules and they're his rules [*laughing*]. Would you like some tea?

She goes to the kitchen.

MANDISA [*following her*]: Yes, love some.

THANDO: You were telling me about yourself.

MANDISA: My mother works for Amnesty International and has done for donkey's years. She met my father in Lagos, Nigeria, where she was working at the Amnesty office. Love at first sight — as my father used to say. They both came to London and got married — I was born ...

THANDO: Any brothers and sisters?

MANDISA: Nope. I am the only child.

THANDO: I had a brother, Luvuyo, not from my mom though, but he died ... he was killed.

MANDISA: During the riots. Yes my daddy told me.

THANDO: Not riots. Student uprisings. My father was devastated. Every morning for months his pillow would be soaked with tears. Always hid his tears from me. Didn't want me to feel that he loved him more than me. I know he did. African men love their sons more than their daughters.

MANDISA: Were the people who killed him ever found?

THANDO: No. It was the police. My father never wanted to find out. Not even during the TRC hearings.

MANDISA: Why? Isn't that what the TRC is there for? We heard a lot about those hearings in London.

THANDO [*taking the teapot, cups, sugar and milk on a tray into the living room*]: He said he had his reasons. Besides … never mind.

MANDISA: What?

THANDO: It doesn't matter.

MANDISA: What doesn't matter?

THANDO: I don't want to upset you.

MANDISA: No, I want to know what you are keeping from me.

THANDO: My father blames your father for Luvuyo's death.

MANDISA: My Father? Why?

THANDO: He'd say that Luvuyo worshipped Uncle Themba. He wanted to be just like him. So when Uncle Themba left the country, he stepped into his shoes, so to speak.

MANDISA: You can't blame someone for somebody else's death just because that person tried to be like his hero.

THANDO: That's what my father says. So remember that … [*uneasy pause. She comes back with the tea*].

Was Uncle Temba as amazing as people here say he was?

MANDISA: Mom says Daddy was one of the ANC cadres studying in Nigeria. When he went to London he became very active. Worked with the Anti-apartheid and the ANC. Mom also did a lot for the movement, I mean exposing the treatment of the detainees and prisoners here in South Africa. Our house was like a halfway house for all South Africans. I grew up listening to all the stories about HOME. The struggle, the memories and the songs. Bra Hugh and Sis Miriam once came to our house. What a gig. They were performing in some venue and so my dad had a few friends around. Then my dad got ill — his heart. I could see he had lost his energy, his drive. He began to long for home.

THANDO: Why did he not come back when Mandela was released?

MANDISA: His job. It was not the right time. Things had to settle down first. They had a life in England, they could not just uproot themselves. Besides they would consider it when my father's health had improved. It never did. It got worse. He called us together about six months ago. He asked us a favour — to ask his brother to bury him at home next to his parents. Closer to his ancestors ... so that's why I am here.

THANDO: He must have been a wonderful man.

MANDISA: Yes he was. Like your father.

THANDO: Yes. Why don't you come with me tomorrow to the amnesty hearing? It's the conclusion of the Cradock case.

MANDISA: I'd love to. Maybe Uncle Sipho can come with us too.

THANDO: No. The funeral arrangements, and besides he has to go to work at the library. He never likes to go to the hearings. Again he says he has his own reasons. He is also awaiting the outcome of the restructuring. They are about to announce the new Chief Librarian. That's another thing that's making him edgy these days.

MANDISA: Why? Is he up for the post?

THANDO: Yes. There is nothing he wants more in his whole life than to be Chief Librarian. That would almost complete his dream.

MANDISA: So what's the problem? My father always said he was the best in the whole country.

THANDO: Yes he is. But you never know with the Government — he has been in that library for thirty-three years. He is 63 years old. They might not want to appoint somebody who might retire within the next two or three years.

MANDISA: That would be so unfair.

THANDO [*taking the tea tray back to the kitchen*]: Is life fair? So, you will come with me. I must also warn you it's not easy to sit through all that horror, listening to confessions. Gruesome details of what they did to our people.

MANDISA [*following* THANDO *to the kitchen*]: Don't worry about me. I am a tough cookie. Hey, what about the man in your life? Boyfriend? Is there one?

THANDO: Yes, Mpho is his name. He is a history teacher. We've been together for about four years.

MANDISA: What are you waiting for? To lose him? [*They laugh.*] Engaged?

THANDO: Sort of. My, you are direct, aren't you?
Tell me about you.

MANDISA: Have you got time? It's a long story.

THANDO: We are going nowhere. I am all ears. I'll get us something to eat. You must be hungry. I've cooked already … for you too.

MANDISA [*looking at the pots on the stove*]: Oh, you mean phutu, morodu and pap and steak?

THANDO: No, that's Johannesburg ... I've prepared chicken, rice and salads. I hope you are not disappointed if it doesn't sound South African. What about you? Anyone in your life?

MANDISA [*going back to the living room*]: Well I've had a couple. My mom always said 'have fun, flirt a little so that you don't feel like you missed out on a lot of the good things in life before you get trapped in marriage'. There was one guy about five years ago ... oh dear. Derek Loxworth, a true gentleman. Very rich family. We were at college together. I loved him very much.

THANDO [*following* MANDISA]: But?

MANDISA: My mother liked him too. But my father saw the whole thing as a passing phase that I was going to get over.

THANDO: He was white?

MANDISA: He was English ... they've always taught me that all people were the same. This whole apartheid thing was ridiculous and unjust, but deep in her heart my mother preferred a man from the West Indies from a very well-to-do family.

THANDO: Your father?

MANDISA: Oh it was simple to him. I must marry a South African black man. Even if it meant I had to look from the children of his exiled South African friends. It was almost incestuous. How so and so's son has grown and become a wonderful young man. How he would make someone a wonderful husband. Even our own black community — the West Africans and West Indians in London — expected us to love and marry within our own. It was as if, like the Afrikaners, we all feared disappearing as a race.

THANDO: What about Derek ... his family?

MANDISA: Oh, he loved me all right ... his family adored me ... especially his sisters. I just could not take the pressure. Everywhere we went, places to eat, to visit, especially those in the black community the sisters were saying 'right on sister', but the brothers were saying — good for you sister. Testing the buoy sister? Him just sowing his seed before him go marry a whitey.

THANDO: Oh but surely there are successful black and white relationships in England?

MANDISA: Of course there are. People are people.

They laugh.

THANDO: And now?

SIPHO *enters from the kitchen.*

MANDISA: Well now, I am fresh on the market. My work has kept me busy preparing for the London Fashion Week. I really want to make a good impression. If things go well, I might get an offer from one of the big fashion houses.

THANDO: Mmn. Wow!

MANDISA: That is why I would like to see as many designers here as possible, before I go back to London. So it's very important that I met this Ms Nandipa in Jo'burg. So please will you come with me?

SIPHO: To where?

THANDO: Tata, you are back. What happened?

SIPHO: There is going to be a funeral on Saturday. Rev Haya reminded me "Umhlaba emhlaben, uthuthu elithuthwini, uthuli elithulwini".

MANDISA: Will somebody ... please.

SIPHO: The Bible says "earth to earth, ashes to ashes and dust to dust". That seems to accommodate ashes too. We just won't have the usual opportunity to see him before the coffin is closed. My uncles are confused, as I am, but they do understand under the present circumstances. Bavumile inkomo ixhelwe ngomgqibelo.

MANDISA: Please Thando?

SIPHO: My uncles have agreed that the ox must be slaughtered on Saturday to clear his passage to the ancestors.

MANDISA: Thank God.

SIPHO: You can say that again. I have already told the undertaker. He has agreed.

MANDISA: So Mom and I are off the hook then?

SIPHO: For the moment. There are a lot of things we still have to talk about young girl. You still have not answered my question … where do you want to take Thando to?

THANDO: Mandisa wants to see some fashion designers. She wants me to go with her to Johannesburg after the funeral, if it's OK with you.

SIPHO: We will talk about that later.

MANDISA [*looking at both of them*]: It's amazing. You do look like my father.

SIPHO [*stunned*]: He was my brother.

Blackout.

'The truth, the whole truth and nothing but the truth'.
Nthati Moshesh (Thando) and John Kani, with Pamela
Nomvete looking on.

Act II

Scene 1

THANDO *and* MANDISA *return from the TRC Amnesty Hearings.* THANDO, *walking in front, opens the kitchen door.* MANDISA *follows — dressed even more stunningly. She looks very upset.*

THANDO: Hello Tata. No sign of him. Anybody home? [*Looking into Sipho's room.*] That's strange he's always here by now.

MANDISA [*opening a bottle of whisky which was in the duty free bag*]: Keep close tabs on him as much as he does on you? Do you?

THANDO: It's just that he is a creature of habit and you get used to people like that. [*Pause.*] Why are you so quiet? You hardly said a thing in the car on the way back.

MANDISA [*pouring herself a shot of whisky*]: No, I am thinking.

THANDO: The hearings make you do that sometimes.

MANDISA: That's all there is to it? No more. We can all go home. All is forgiven. Somebody died for God's sake. Someone is guilty.

THANDO: You don't understand. That's how we chose to do it. That's the option we took.

MANDISA: Then make me understand. Pretend I am an idiot. Explain it to me. A man sends a parcel bomb to two women and a child. It blows their guts out and he is not guilty of any crime.

THANDO: It's not as simple as that. There are conditions to be met.

MANDISA: Damn you, Thando. This man murdered Ruth First in cold blood. In the most cowardly way. Just because Joe Slovo was considered Public Enemy No. 1 by the apartheid government. A terrorist as they called him. Who the fuck gave Craig Williamson the right to murder his wife? And what did Mrs Schoon and her daughter do? How could those two women and a child overthrow the white racist government of South Africa? Remember what the lawyer said of him. He's South Africa's super spy. South Africa's secret agent abroad, with a license to kill, whom in his illustrious career, could only boast of killing two women and a child.

THANDO: Mandisa, we had a choice. We could have gone for revenge. We could have gone for Nuremberg-style trials but how would that have made us different from them?

MANDISA: For what in return?

THANDO: Peace, stability, reconciliation.

MANDISA: You mean international reconciliation. They were so dying for international approval that they sold out. Did anyone of them think about the people? Did someone warn them that the people might want that revenge?

THANDO: We have a country to rebuild. A nation to take care of. An economy to grow, jobs to create, houses to build, clinics, hospitals, schools and our lives. Where would revenge get us except more violence? Besides we did not want to give those bastards the honour of taking up arms against us in their defence and call it a legitimate struggle. There was one Struggle, the struggle for liberation, our Struggle.

MANDISA: Then why is Craig Williamson a free man? He committed murder.

THANDO: Because according to the rules and requirements for amnesty …

MANDISA: He disclosed all? Yes. He told us nothing new except that he sent the parcel bombs. Who gave the order? Do we know that? Does that make him innocent?

THANDO: No, it does not. He met the conditions set for amnesty.

MANDISA: Then why was there an outcry against him receiving amnesty? Why was everybody angry?

THANDO: Not everybody was.

MANDISA: Joe Slovo is. Ruth's children are. I am.

THANDO: How do you know that Joe Slovo is?

MANDISA: Let's dig up his grave shall we. Let's open the coffin and see if that skull is smiling.

THANDO: Joe Slovo said before he died he would never accept the granting of general amnesty. He wanted to know who killed his wife and why. It was personal to him. Now he knows. Now we all know.

MANDISA: But somebody must be made to pay.

THANDO: Typical of someone sitting 6 000 miles away. In a comfortable house in London, observing the whole situation with a pair of binoculars. You and your periodic amnesia, choosing to remember and forget as you wish.

The policemen who killed the Pebco 3 were refused amnesty. You were there today. Derby-Lewis and Janus Walus are rotting in jail for the murder of Chris Hani. No, your anger is selective. We, who stayed here. We who witnessed first hand the police brutality. We who every Saturday buried hundreds of our young brothers and sisters shot by the police, dying in detention, dying because of orchestrated black on black violence, accept the TRC process. You have no right to question that. Mandela spent

27 years in prison. Is he asking for someone to be sent to Robben Island to spend years there as a payback? If all those who suffered can forgive, then so can you. If our President can ask us to work for a better life for all of our people, so can you

MANDISA [*going into the kitchen and pouring herself another shot of whisky*]: Thando, you must at least admit it does look too easy.

SIPHO *enters — sees the whisky bottle, puts the lid back on and listens.*

THANDO: People from overseas always oversimplify our situation. We would never have achieved our democracy without all our people, black and white, coming together to overthrow apartheid.

MANDISA: Oh please! That's the attitude my father always talked about. "The generosity of the African people." I call it giving in too easily.

SIPHO [*who has been standing unnoticed at the living room door*]: I call it African humanity!

THANDO: Daddy.

MANDISA: How long have you been standing there?

SIPHO: Does it matter? It is called African humanity, ubuntu, not generosity.

MANDISA: You know it's very rude to eavesdrop on other people's conversations.

SIPHO: This is my house. I do not eavesdrop. I listen and hear what people say in my house. What part of this conversation did you not want to me hear?

THANDO: Where have you been? You are almost three hours late.

SIPHO: I've been drinking at Sky's shebeen.

THANDO: But you don't drink. You haven't had a drink since Luvuyo died.

SIPHO: I do now. And why did your father not come back in 1994? It's now 2000.

THANDO: That's enough Daddy.

MANDISA: My father had his reasons.

SIPHO: Oh yes. I am sure he had his reasons.

THANDO: I said that's enough, both of you. [*Pause.*] By the way, what happened at work today, Daddy?

SIPHO: Everything happened. Everything.

THANDO: Did you … Did you get the job?

SIPHO: No I did not get the job.

THANDO: I am so sorry Daddy.

SIPHO: No, don't be.

THANDO: So who did get the job then?

SIPHO: Some young person from Johannesburg. To shake up the library. Make it run like a business. A business! Even make money to pay for itself. A public library, for God's sake!

THANDO: My father has been running that library for the past six years. Successfully I might add. It has become the most used library in the Eastern Cape. Even Mrs Potgieter publicly admitted that they could not have achieved that without my father. She even recommended that my father would be the best person to take over from her.

MANDISA: So what was the problem then?

SIPHO: My age.

MANDISA: What has your age got to do with it.

SIPHO: I am sixty-three years old. They could not give this important position to an old man who is about to retire in two years' time.

THANDO: And this younger person? What experience has he got? Did you see him?

SIPHO: No, I did not see him. His qualifications? I am not sure … all I hear is that he is from exile or something.

MANDISA: Is that a qualification?

SIPHO: These days it is.

MANDISA: Bullshit!

THANDO: I am sorry Daddy. You deserved that job. You've waited for it all your life.

SIPHO: It's OK Thando. It's done. There is nothing we can do about it.

MANDISA: Are you going to let him take what is rightfully yours?

SIPHO: Yes, yes. People always take things from me. It's been like that all my life.

THANDO: I think you should go to sleep now Daddy.

SIPHO: No! I've been asleep too long. People have always taken from me. When I finished high school I could not go to university. My father had no money. So I had to look for a job. I got one. Spilkin & Spilkin Attorneys wanted a clerk. I told Mr Spilkin Senior that I actually wanted to be a lawyer. I would love to do articles. He said 'Of course, but not now'. They had two young white boys who were with them and as soon as they graduated in three years time I could start. In the meantime I could work for them as a clerk. 'We are glad to have you on board, Sifo'. 'No, Mr Spilkin, It is not Sifo, Sipho.' 'What's the difference,' he asked. 'Sifo means a disease, Mr Spilkin, and Sipho means a gift and that is my name.' Like a deliberate curse, that's what he called me from that day onwards. Sifo, a disease.

THANDO: I've never heard this story before.

MANDISA: How long did you stay there?

SIPHO: For three years. When I told Mr Spilkin that I was ready to start my articles he said he was very sorry they had already decided to take two new white articled clerks. Anyway I was doing a very good job now, he said.

SIPHO: Then I heard that they were looking for someone, someone black, at the Port Elizabeth Public Library to train as an assistant librarian. I left Spilkin & Spilkin Attorneys. I got the job at the library. Mrs Meyers was very impressed with my English. She said with such good English I would go far in her library. So Spilkin & Spilkin Attorneys took my one chance. I really wanted to be a lawyer.

MANDISA: And where was my father all this time?

SIPHO: By this time Themba had finished high school. My father somehow found the money to send Themba to Fort Hare University. I was very happy for him but I was also sad and angry. I did not understand where my father got the money now. I found out later that my father had cashed in his Old Mutual Life Insurance policy. Took the money and sent Themba to university to study for a B.Comm.

My father could only pay for boarding and tuition. I paid for everything else. His clothes — and he only wore the best. His food and pocket money. The course was three years. He took five wonderful years. The best holiday Themba ever had, and at my expense.

My mother died before Themba graduated. I cried. She was the only one who ever said to me she loved me. My father openly favoured Themba and it hurt. Themba graduated a year later and never got a job. All that university education for nothing. All wasted on Themba and he never cared. Both my father and I continued to support him.

33

He goes to the kitchen, grabs the whisky bottle and tries to open it.

MANDISA [*following*]: This is ridiculous.

THANDO [*grabbing the bottle from him*]: Why? Why did you continue to support him?

MANDISA: I don't believe a word of it. My father told us he graduated at the top of his class. Are you telling me that my father was useless, never took care of his family? That's a lie! I refuse to listen to anymore of this drunken drivel.

SIPHO: Shut up! [*He returns to the living room* — THANDO *and* MANDISA *follow.*] Because he was my brother. He was family. I started working at the library. The first thing Mrs Meyers did was to ask me to enrol at UNISA to do a Diploma in Librarian Management. I passed with distinction within two years. I was happy at last and earned good money to support my dad and Themba of course as we all lived in this house.

THANDO: And Luvuyo.

SIPHO: His mother is another story. I raised Luvuyo myself. Themba loved him very much. While I was at work, it was Themba who looked after him and for that I will always be grateful to him.

MANDISA: At least there was something my father did that you approved of.

SIPHO: One day I was busy unpacking a new shipment of books we had received. Among them were some books by African writers. Mrs Meyers put me in charge of the African section, which had three shelves next to the comic book stand, a little outside the main section of the library, just opposite the small Afrikaans section. I did not care. I knew the books were there and I was in charge! Mrs Meyers left for England, her husband died. She made me her assistant before she left. That is how I became the Assistant Chief Librarian. I will never forget her for that.

He coughs.

THANDO: Let me get you a glass of water.

Exits.

MANDISA: Did you love my father?
SIPHO: He was my brother. He was family.
MANDISA: Did you hate my father?
SIPPHO: Don't be silly. I can't hate my brother.
MANDISA: I think you are evading the question. My father always spoke about you with some sadness. He said there was some unfinished business between the two of you. What was it?

THANDO *enters with a glass and a jug of water. Pours.*

SIPHO: Thank you Thando. Yesterday you asked me about your mother.
THANDO: Are you sure you want to talk about her? Is it the drink?
SIPHO: It's not the drink. It's time. One day a young lady came into the library. I jumped out of my little office to help her. I knew if Mrs Potgieter saw her first, she would tell her politely to get out of the library. The library was not allowed to serve blacks in those days.

I met her right at the door. She told me that she had not come to the library to borrow a book. She actually came to see where I worked. She always sat a few seats behind me in the bus every morning on the way to work. I always had a book in my hand. A different one every week. So she came to ask me if I would lend her the books before I returned them to the library.

I could not talk for a second. It seemed a lifetime. 'Of course', I said. 'Anything for you. I mean that it would be no problem at all.' For the first time something inside was awakened, something that was so deep in my heart that I could not even know it existed. A warm feeling came over me. My eyes got warm. I knew if I blinked tears would run down. It was as if she was aware of what was going on inside me. She saved me the embarrassment. She turned and walked away. 'I hope to see you again some time,' I said. Without turning she answered 'I hope to see you too.' She disappeared into the crowd walking down the street.

THANDO: Oh Tata!

SIPHO: I did not even ask for her name. Where she stayed. But I knew we would meet again. It was meant. My mistake was to ask Themba if he knew such a girl. Your father had an anthology of every beautiful woman who ever walked the streets of New Brighton. Themba knew her immediately. He also said she was not my type. Themba knew those things.

THANDO: What did he mean by that?

SIPHO: She would find me too serious. Oh! he was wrong! When we met the second time that was it. We fell in love, just like that. Within six months we were married. We were happy. Themba liked her. My father liked her too and I was in love and happy! That was your mother, Sindiswa Makhapela. The most beautiful woman I've ever known.

THANDO: So that was my mother?

SIPHO: For three years we could not have a child. The doctors said we were both OK. It's just that my sperm count was not high enough, but at the same time not too low either or something like that. So there was a 50/50 chance. In the fourth year, she fell pregnant and you were born and I was so happy!

MANDISA: I did not know you were a bit of a romantic. Daddy never told me that.

SIPHO: There are a lot of things that your father never told you about me it seems.

MANDISA: What are you going to do about the job at the library?

THANDO: Daddy can take the package now. The early retirement as they call it.

SIPHO: Or remain again for the seventh time as Assistant Chief Librarian. Get a gold wristwatch and a small farewell function in the basement of the library and then fuck off.

THANDO: Daddy … you are swearing!

SIPHO: Yes, I am. All I wanted was to be the Chief Librarian. Is that too much to ask?

MANDISA: Sixty-three years is not old at all. How old was Mandela when he became President?

SIPHO: That's different. Mandela was on Robben Island. He was also president of the ANC. Age did not count. [*The telephone rings.*] I'll get that. Hello ngubani lowo. Oh Reverend. Uxolo mongameli. The obituary? I forgot about that. I am coming over.

Exits.

MANDISA: Wow, what a pack of stories!

THANDO: He has never spoken so much before. I am worried about him.

MANDISA: You've never seen him drunk before?

THANDO: NO! Not since the death of Luvuyo.

MANDISA: He'll be all right. He will sober up. Tell me, did he like my father?

THANDO: He's never spoken about him before today

MANDISA: Of course he did. Maybe I should buy him another bottle.

She goes to the kitchen, takes the whisky bottle and pours another glass.

THANDO: Stop it, Mandisa!

They laugh.

MANDISA [*going back to the living room*]: Hey, what are we doing tonight. Why don't you call your boyfriend Mpho and we all go out for dinner tonight.

THANDO: I have to prepare something for my dad first.

MANDISA: He can take care of himself, can't he?

THANDO: No, I have to. Anyway Mpho knows that I am not available until after the funeral tomorrow.

MANDISA: Surely there is nothing wrong with us going for a quick bite at a restaurant. I also want to meet your boyfriend. What's his telephone number?

She picks up the phone.

THANDO: Put the phone down Mandisa.

MANDISA: Give me the number. I don't think anyone would mind if we went out tonight.

THANDO: And when my father comes back and we are not here? What if some people come to enquire about the funeral? No, we can't go anywhere.

MANDISA: What is all the fuss about. The whole funeral business is just ceremonial.

THANDO: Not to us. We have a funeral tomorrow. Put that phone down.

MANDISA [*putting down the phone*]: Well I am going out tonight. I've spent the whole day listening to sad stories.

THANDO: Your father's funeral is tomorrow Mandisa. Show some respect and mourn for him.

MANDISA: No one tells me what to do with my life. I am going out.

THANDO: You are in my father's house. We are mourning the death of my uncle. Show some respect for our traditions. This is not England.

MANDISA: My father did say that his brother was a bit conservative. Thando, you are young. You don't have to do what pleases him.

THANDO: This has nothing to do with my father. It's what I want to do. That's what this community expects of us and you are going to do the same.

MANDISA: OK. I will stay. What are we going to eat? Can I help?

THANDO: That sounds better. I'll whip up something quickly.

Exits to kitchen.

MANDISA: Listen. After the funeral why don't you come with me to Johannesburg? I've decided I am going to stay for a few extra days. You know I have to see a few designers. Look we can spend a week there together. Please say yes!

THANDO: Nandipa *is* the best. I have one of her designs. I will show you. I bought one of her dresses when we went to the Rand Easter Show with Mpho last year. Wait, let me show you.

Exits to put on the designer dress.

39

The phone rings.

THANDO [*from the bedroom*]: Answer it, Mandisa.

MANDISA: Hello, Makhaya residence. Can I help you ? No … He is not in. He has just walked out. Yes … I am sure he will be back soon. Thando is not available. Can I take a message? Yes. Mrs [*spelling it out*] P O T G…G I E T E R. Thank you. I will tell him. He is all right. I will. Thank you. Yes, I am his niece from London. Thanks.

THANDO [*from the bedroom*]: Who was that?

MANDISA [*mispronouncing the name*]: A Mrs Potgiator.

THANDO: Mrs Potgieter! That's my father's former Chief Librarian. What did she say?

MANDISA: She has just heard that Uncle Sipho did not get the post. She says to tell him how sorry she is. She also wanted to know if he was OK. [THANDO *enters, wearing the designer dress.*] My God! I have never seen anything like this in my life!

THANDO: Isn't it beautiful? I have only worn it once.

MANDISA: It is divine! Now I know I must see Nandipa! Turn around. Wow! I don't know what to say. It's beautiful! It's stunning!

THANDO: This is the only one of her creations I could afford. There were many others there that just blew my mind.

MANDISA: You must come with me. I insist.

THANDO: My father … I don't think he would agree.

MANDISA: Your father can take care of himself. Can't he? What will happen if Mpho decides to marry you? Are you going to say 'No, I can't leave my father alone'? Grow up Thando! If he can't make it alone, that's not your problem. It's his, not yours.

THANDO: Look, I want to go.

MANDISA: So you are coming with me?

THANDO: Yes ... yes!

MANDISA: Thando, I have an even better idea. The schools are closed. Aren't they?

THANDO: For another three weeks.

SIPHO *enters the kitchen unnoticed.*

MANDISA: Come with me to London. We will go together to the London Fashion Week. My father always said he wished you could come to London.

THANDO: I am so excited, and confused at the same time. What about Mpho?

MANDISA: It is only for three weeks Thando! One week in Johannesburg and two weeks in London. That can't change his mind about you, if he really loves you.

THANDO: I know that. Mpho is not the problem. I am not sure that my father would agree.

MANDISA: To Hell with your father! It's your life! If Mpho doesn't mind, why do you care about your father? Tell him you are going away with me to London for two weeks. It's not like you are going forever! Even if you were it would still be your decision.

SIPHO: Well spoken, Mandisa! Like father, like daughter!

MANDISA: Oh, not again! I think I should buy you squeaky shoes.

THANDO: Look Daddy, it's not like that! I haven't said I would go. I would never go without your permission and blessing!

MANDISA: Blessing yes, permission no. It is up to you, Thando, if you want to go with me. You are old enough to make decisions for yourself.

THANDO: Daddy, you caught the tail end of the conversation. Mandisa wants to spend next week in Johannesburg seeing some important designers.

SIPHO: And now you are dressed to go?

THANDO: You mean this dress? No. I was just showing Mandisa one of Nandipa's designs. She wondered if I could go with her to Johannesburg next week. After the funeral, of course.

SIPHO: And London?

THANDO: No. Yes. I mean one thing led to another. We were just talking. I had not yet agreed that I would go with her, even to Johannesburg. I was still going to ask you first.

MANDISA: Ask him now Thando.

THANDO: Stay out of this Mandisa.

MANDISA: Ask him now.

THANDO: Shut up Mandisa!

MANDISA: Then I will ask him for you. Uncle Sipho would you please be so kind as to allow Thando to go with me to Johannesburg next week since she is still on holiday from school?

SIPHO: No.

MANDISA: What do you mean No. Should you at least not ask her what she thinks?

SIPHO: No.

MANDISA: No, you don't care what she thinks, or No, she can't go.

SIPHO: No! No!

THANDO: Daddy. I think Mandisa is right. You should ask me if I want to go. You can't just say No without hearing me first. After all she is my sister, isn't she? Your brother's daughter. She is family, isn't she?

SIPHO: My answer is No. And it is final!

MANDISA: What do you say Thando?

THANDO: I will talk to my father about this later.

MANDISA: No. Now. You can't allow him to run your life like this. Are you coming with me to Johannesburg and London next week?

THANDO: Stop it Mandisa!

MANDISA: No. I want to know now. You have to tell me now. Are you coming?

THANDO: I can't answer you now.

MANDISA: I don't understand. You were so excited about this trip just a few minutes ago. Just before your father arrived. You know something? My father always hoped that some day we would meet. He always said that life was tough in South Africa. That you should travel and see the world, expand your horizons, that you would see that the world is a beautiful place. Not always war, hatred and violence. He always wished, if he could, to bring you to London. Both of you.

SIPHO: I don't want to go to London.

MANDISA: Then at least let Thando go.

SIPHO: I said No.

THANDO: Give me one good reason why you don't want me to go. One reason and I will not go.

SIPHO: Because I love you.

THANDO: I've always known that. That's not the reason.

SIPHO: Because you are my only child.

THANDO: How will going with Mandisa change that?

SIPHO: Oh it will.

MANDISA: That's rubbish. I don't want to take her away from you. I just want to take her to Johannesburg and London.

SIPHO: The taking never stops. I've always known this would happen one day.

THANDO: I don't know what you are talking about. I am still waiting for one good reason why you don't want me to go.

MANDISA: Forget it Thando. You can stay, if that will make him happy. I am a little surprised though, because my father said that Uncle Sipho always put other people's happiness first. His family's happiness came first, even before his own. Well it's obvious then that Uncle Sipho has changed.

SIPHO: What else did your father say about me?

THANDO [*going into the bedroom to change the dress*]: It doesn't matter any more.

SIPHO: I still want to know. What else did your father tell you about me?

MANDISA: He said you were very conservative.

SIPHO: You mean dull.

MANDISA: That too. No sense of humour. You took life too seriously. You and your library. All that ever mattered to you was that library. Well, Uncle Sipho, you've lost the library. You did not become the Chief Librarian.

THANDO [*from the bedroom*]: That's enough Mandisa!

MANDISA: So give it up and live! You are not dead yet. Let Thando live too! She cannot spend the rest of her life looking after you. Let her go. Let her marry Mpho.

THANDO: Shut up Mandisa!

MANDISA: Let her come with me to Johannesburg and London. You are not too old to find someone, someone to love, like you loved Thando's mother.

THANDO: That's enough!

MANDISA: No Thando, my father was right.

SIPHO: Let me tell you about your father.

THANDO: Stop it Mandisa.

MANDISA: No, no, no. I want to know what he has to say about my father.

THANDO: Shut up, Mandisa!

MANDISA: My father was cremated last week. I brought his ashes to be buried next to his parents. If Uncle Sipho does not want to do that I am not going to beg him. I will ask somebody to show me where his parents are buried and I will scatter the ashes between them and go home. My father was right. Uncle Sipho was jealous because my father was a hero of the Struggle.

SIPHO: If your father was a hero of the Struggle why did he not come back when the exiles came back? Why was he not part of the Kempton Park delegation that negotiated with the apartheid government? Did he ever tell you why he could not come back?

MANDISA: He was not well. He wanted to be well first, then he would come back. He did not want to come back a sick man.

SIPHO: He preferred to come back a dead man in that thing. How convenient.

THANDO [*coming back into the living room*]: Stop it! Both of you! I've made up my mind. I am going to Johannesburg with you Mandisa. With or without your permission, Daddy. About London, that is another matter. I'll let you know later.

SIPHO: Even if he is dead he is still taking from me.

THANDO: What do you mean? Why do you keep saying that? What is this 'taking' about?

They sit.

SIPHO: When my father died in 1987 Themba could not come to the funeral. It was too dangerous for him to come back. The UDF took over my father's funeral.

MANDISA: Why?

SIPHO: It was Comrade Themba's wishes. They turned my father's funeral into a political rally.There were twelve speakers. One after the other, talking about Themba's father. I sat there like a stranger. I paid for the coffin. I paid for all the funeral arrangements. I even paid for the food they were all eating. But I was just Comrade Themba's brother.

They whisked his coffin away, carried it shoulder high and ran with it all the way to the cemetery. My aunts and uncles could not keep up with them. The police were all over. It was chaos. Kids were toyi-toying, taunting the police to shoot them. It was like the day they buried my son. I ran behind the coffin. At the graveyard I was not even the first to throw the soil on the coffin. No, it was the delegates first. The songs went on forever.

The police could not take it any more. They fired teargas right at the graveyard. People began to run. Old ladies coughing and crying. I stood there, right over my father's coffin. I did not run. I wanted the police to shoot me right there. I had had enough of it all. When the dust settled, the police gone, the comrades gone, it was just Rev Haya and the undertaker and me still standing there. The teargas did not affect us at all it seemed. Rev Haya said a prayer and I buried my father. I alone filled the grave with the soil, planted the cross with his name, date of birth and date of death. Lala ngoxolo mfo wase Ma Cireni. I then said a little prayer and said goodbye to my father. I apologised for the chaos. I was very angry at Themba for doing that to my father.

MANDISA: This is absolute crap! I am not going to listen to this!

SIPHO: For once do as I ask. Shut up! And you say I was jealous of him! For what! For being an activist. Yes! A political activist who never threw one stone at the police, who never blew up any police station. Themba could talk. He was always amongst the speakers, at the Great Centenary Hall, at the Dan Qege Stadium. He always said what the people wanted to hear. Calling for stay aways when he himself was unemployed. No, let me put it this way, when he himself never had a job in his life. He supported the students' school boycott when he did not have a child at school. Called for consumer boycotts when he knew who bought the food he ate. An executive member of the Workers' Executive Committee. How? I do not know since he never had a job. Proposed rent boycotts when he did not have a house. He stayed with me in my house. Themba went to these gatherings because they were his hunting ground for other people's wives. Oh he was famous for that! There was not a single woman who had not slept with Comrade Themba. Wives, girlfriends, Themba made no distinction. I always worried that someone, some husband or boyfriend, was going to kill Themba even before the Security Police could. That is why I still blame him for the death of my son.

MANDISA: That's the most despicable thing to say of your own brother. He loved Luvuyo.

SIPHO: The last time I saw my son alive was when he was on his way to a little girl's funeral. He was a poet you see. He use to recite his poems at political rallies, funerals and special occasions. I told him not to go. I knew there was going to be trouble. I could see death in his eyes. He looked at me and said that Uncle Themba was right, I was a coward. He left. I never saw him alive again. I loved him too much. I wanted him to live. I did not want him to die. Did that make me a coward?

THANDO: Daddy, please.

SIPHO: In your father's eyes I was.

MANDISA: What are you saying about my father? Are you saying he was a total fake? He was no hero?

SIPHO: No. He was involved. He was in the Struggle, but on his terms. He got what he wanted from the Struggle — money, women and fame.

THANDO: Then why did he leave the country? Everybody says if he had stayed the police would have killed him. So what are you saying?

SIPHO: Themba left because I ... we had a fight.

THANDO: What!

MANDISA: Yes. My father once told us about a terrible fight you had with him.

THANDO: Yes. I also had something like that from my aunt. She said my mother knew what the fight was about. What happened, Daddy? Why did she leave?

SIPHO: I told you. She stopped loving me, that's all. She had to leave.

THANDO: She had to leave? What do you mean? Why? No one in the family ever wanted to talk about my mother. Everyone always says 'Oh your mother, Thando, she was very beautiful. Your father loved her very much,' and nothing more! I was eighteen months old when she left. No mother can forget her baby forever. Not a letter, or a message from her to me. Durban is not in another country. Do you know where she is? Do you know why she left me? Me, Daddy, not you! Why she left me! I want to know. Now!

MANDISA: What did my father do to you? What happened between the two of you?

SIPHO: He never told you?

MANDISA: No! This is crap. I can't stay here any longer. I am going out to dinner. Even if I have to go alone.

Both women start to exit.

SIPHO: Stop! No one leaves this house. You want to know the truth? You want to know why I fought your father? You want to know why your mother left me? Left an eighteen-month-old baby in my hands and walked away and never came back?

THANDO *and* **MANDISA**: Yes!

SIPHO: Themba was sleeping with my wife.

MANDISA: What!

SIPHO: Your father was sleeping with my wife, your mother!

THANDO: No! No!

MANDISA: This has gone too far! It's not true, it's not true!!

MANDISA: I don't believe you! My father would never do such a thing. He was loyal to mother — always.

SIPHO: That's what you think. Themba was good at making people believe in him.

THANDO: Oh my God!

MANDISA [*sobbing openly*]: No, no. Not my father.

SIPHO: The truth, the whole truth and nothing but the truth, so help me God. That's what you've asked for. So sit down and take it like the adults you both claim to be. I came home early from work that day. I wasn't feeling well. I had the flu. My head was pounding. When I got here, I opened the kitchen door with my own keys. The radio was playing too loud. The radio was right here on this sideboard. I turned the volume down. Then I heard your

49

mother laugh. I went towards her, looked into the bedroom and there they were. On my bed. Both naked and making love. They both looked up as they felt my presence. Your mother screamed. Themba dropped his face into the pillow in total shock and shame. I walked out. I did not say a word. I just kept walking and walking. When I came back they were both gone. I never saw them again.

THANDO: All these years we have lived together you've kept this in your heart, alone. You've never shared with me, your own daughter. Why?

SIPHO: How could I tell you. It was best to say nothing.

THANDO: So Uncle Themba took my mother from you?

SIPHO: He took everything.

THANDO: No, not everything. I am here with you. I am not going with Mandisa.

SIPHO [*pushing her away*]: No Thando. You must leave with Mandisa.

THANDO: I am staying here with you.

SIPHO: I do not need you anymore.

THANDO: How long had Uncle Themba been sleeping with my mother?

SIPHO [*pushing her away*]: I do not know. Please do not ask me that.

THANDO: For how long?

MANDISA: What does it matter for how long? It happened. Leave it now. Can't you see you are hurting your father more by these questions?

THANDO: I want to know for how long, Daddy?

SIPHO [*bursting into tears*]: For three years.

THANDO: Oh my God! No! It can't be. You mean there could be a possibility that I could be ... No. It's not possible!

SIPHO: I told you to leave it alone. I begged you to stop. No, you wanted to go on. You wanted to know the truth.

THANDO: Yes! But tell me I am wrong! Tell me it is not so! I can't take this any more.

She exits, sobbing.

MANDISA: So she could be my sister?

SIPHO: Yes. She could be. She could also be my daughter. I found a letter written by your father, asking her to keep the baby because it could be mine. So, take her from me. Just like your father took everything from me and get out!

She exits.

SIPHO: So, you win again Themba. I am still dull. Nothing good is for me. I am still at the library and I am not even the Chief Librarian and will never be. If this country was free, I used to say, I would be the Chief Librarian. I watched the release of Nelson Mandela on TV and I said to myself 'my time has come'. I was 57 years old when I voted on 27 April 1994. I put them in power. I made Nelson Mandela the first democratically elected president of this country. I was 62 years old when I voted again in 1999. Nobody said I was too old. How come I am not old to put them in power but then suddenly I am too old to be empowered? This Government owes me. I have been loyal to them. Why could they not make me the Chief Librarian just for two years? Two years only. That's not too much to ask. Is it?

I was part of the Struggle. I too suffered as a black person. I went to the marches like everyone else. I might not have been detained. I might not have been on Robben Island. I did not leave this country, but I suffered too. The thousands that attended those funerals on Saturdays, that was me. The thousands that were tear gassed, sjamboked by the police, mauled by Alsatian dogs, that was me. When

Bishop Tutu led thousands through the streets of white Port Elizabeth, that was me. I WAS THOSE THOUSANDS! I too deserved some recognition, didn't I?

No! No more! It's payback time. The taking stops right here and now. I want everything back, Themba. I want my wire double decker bus now. I want it back. It was mine. Mom and Dad are not here now to speak for you. I want my blazer back. It was mine. I want my wife back. She was mine. She loved me, not you. Do you hear me? I want my daughter back. She is mine. She's my baby, not yours. She is the one thing you cannot take away from me. Not even now. Thando is mine.

THANDO *and* MANDISA *come back into the room.*

THANDO: Yes, I am your daughter. Nothing is going to change that.

SIPHO: The taking must stop. I want my son back. De Klerk must come back from wherever he is. He has to tell me who killed my son and why. I want to know what this government is going to do about it.

THANDO: It's not too late. The hearings are still on. No case is closed.

SIPHO: I am not talking about the TRC and your amnesty hearings. I want to know now what the government, what the police are going to do about it. I want the Minister of Safety and Security to appoint a senior investigating officer to re-open Luvuyo's case. To investigate and to report back to the Attorney General that he has found the white policeman who shot my son.

MANDISA: And then what?

THANDO: What good will that do now? Will that bring Luvuyo back?

SIPHO: I want him put in jail. He must be charged with the murder of Luvuyo Makhaya, the son of Mr Sipho Makhaya.

MANDISA: Yes.

SIPHO: He must be kept in jail for months awaiting trial. The case must be heard by a black judge.

MANDISA: Yes.

SIPHO: He must have a good lawyer who must try to prove that the killing of the deceased was politically motivated.

MANDISA: Exactly.

SIPHO: He must fail to prove that. The judge must not accept that as a good defence. The judge must find, without any doubt, that he killed my son deliberately. He killed him because he hated blacks. Then he must be found guilty. He must be sentenced to serve time in prison for killing my son.

MANDISA: Yes, that's more like it and for a long time!

SIPHO: A day, a month, a year or ten years. I don't care. As long as he knows that he has been found guilty of the crime he committed. He must be taken to St. Alban's Prison outside Port Elizabeth, like any other murderer. At the prison reception they must shave his head, strip him naked and search to see if he has hidden anything up his arse.

THANDO: Stop it, Daddy!

SIPHO: No, not yet. I haven't finished yet. They must give him a prison khaki shirt and a pair of prison khaki shorts. No shoes. One grey blanket and a mat to sleep on. The following day he must wake up in his cell in prison, knowing that he is serving time for killing my son. Then and only then can he apply for amnesty.

THANDO: Will you forgive him then?

SIPHO: Not forgive him. I will agree that he be given amnesty because 'he has disclosed all'.

MANDISA [*to* THANDO]: Thank you.

THANDO: Will that make you happy?

SIPHO: You don't get it, do you? This whole fucking country doesn't get it. It's not about me. It's not about me being happy or not, forgiving him or not. It's about justice. That's what it's about. So that my soul can rest. So that I can say to myself 'yes, justice has been done'.

MANDISA: What about my father?

SIPHO: What about your father?

THANDO: I told her you blame Uncle Themba for Luvuyo's death.

SIPHO: I still do. But I am not talking about that now. I want everything that was mine given back to me now. I want my job. I am the Chief Librarian of the Port Elizabeth Public Library. I don't care what the Department says about my age. If on Monday I am not sitting in the Chief Librarian's office with my name on the door, there will be no office for anyone, and no library for Port Elizabeth.

THANDO: What are you going to do?

SIPHO: I am going to blow it up!

MANDISA: Great!

SIPHO: No! I am going to burn it down!

MANDISA: Even better! NO! You are drunk! You don't really mean that, do you?

SIPHO: Yes, yes I do! I am dead serious. I am going to burn it down. I am going to watch all those books burn and light up the sky.

THANDO: You will be arrested.

MANDISA: They will say you are mad.

SIPHO: That's even better. I will prove to them that my crime too was politically motivated. They will have to grant me amnesty. They have no choice. I qualify, don't I Thando? You know these things.

THANDO: This is silly. You are going to do no such thing! Stop laughing, Mandisa!

SIPHO: How are you going to stop me?

THANDO: I'll tell the police to stop you.

SIPHO: You will inform the police about me? You will sell me out?

THANDO: It's not selling out. We will stop you.

SIPHO: Why?

THANDO: Because what you want to do is wrong.

SIPHO: What they did to me was wrong too. Why do you want to stop me?

THANDO: Because I love you. I don't want to lose you!

MANDISA: She's right. I love you too, Uncle Sipho. You are the only father I have now.

Pause.

SIPHO: You see what you have done to me Themba. Even when you are dead, ashes in that vase, you are still making my life a misery. Why? Why Themba?

MANDISA: Because he loved you!

THANDO: It's true, Daddy. People always hurt those they love the most. Especially family.

SIPHO: It that true, Mandisa? Did he ever say that? Did he ever say he loved me?

MANDISA: Yes. You can phone my mother right now. During his last days that's all he talked about. You, Uncle Sipho.

SIPHO: I've waited so long to hear that.

THANDO: So you don't blame him for Luvuyo's death?

SIPHO: In my heart I've always known it wasn't his fault. Blaming him just gave me a reason to be angry with him and it felt good. It was the only way I could deal with Luvuyo's death.

THANDO: So you forgive him?

SIPHO: I forgave Themba long ago. All I wanted was for your father to come home, stand in front of me and say 'I am sorry, my brother'.

THANDO: For everything.

SIPHO: Yes. For everything.

THANDO: Including my mother.

SIPHO: The affair. I blame myself.

THANDO: And my mother?

SIPHO: I love her. I will always love her. She is your mother.

MANDISA: For what it's worth Uncle Sipho I am sorry for what my father did to you, to our family. I want you to believe me.

SIPHO: If I can forgive all the white people for what they did to us in this country, how can I not forgive my own brother.

MANDISA: You mean that, Uncle Sipho?

SIPHO: Yes, a man is much more than the worst thing he's ever done.

THANDO: Tell him now, say that to him.

SIPHO: Who?

THANDO: Uncle Themba.

SIPHO: How I wish I could.

THANDO: You've always told me that the dead are living. They are among us all the time. We can talk to them any time we want.

SIPHO: Yes it's true I believe that

THANDO [*pointing at the urn with the ashes*]: Then what are you waiting for? There he is.

MANDISA: Uncle Sipho, can I ask you something?

SIPHO: Anything.

MANDISA: Promise me that you will answer me truthfully.

SIPHO: I do. Yes.

MANDISA: Honestly?

SIPHO: Now you are making me nervous. I said I will answer you truthfully.

MANDISA: All the things you said about my father, are they true?

SIPHO: About your father and Thando's mother?

MANDISA: No, about him being a political activist, that he was no hero, about him being a fake, a liar and a womaniser. Is all that true?

SIPHO: He was a political activist. Everybody loved him. It was always Themba this, Comrade Themba that. I was angry at him for that.

THANDO: A little jealous maybe?

SIPHO: Yes I was jealous. Very jealous. It was Themba all the time. What about me? I was there too. I kept the family together. I hated him for that. [*Pause.*] Your father is a hero of the Struggle. If he had stayed the police would have killed him as they did my son.

MANDISA: Thank you Uncle Sipho.

He kisses her on the forehead.

SIPHO: I wish I knew what he looked like now.

MANDISA [*going into Thando's room*]: I've got something for you.

THANDO: Can I ask you something too?

SIPHO: About your mother?

THANDO: No, you've already told me everything about her and I am very happy about that.

SIPHO: What then?

THANDO: The Library. Are you really going to burn it down? [MANDISA *laughs*]. You weren't serious were you?

SIPHO: No Thando. You know me better than that. I can never burn books.

THANDO: About Luvuyo. The policeman who shot him. Do you forgive him?

Long pause — SIPHO *does not answer.*

MANDISA *comes back into the living room and gives* SIPHO *a photograph of her father.*

SIPHO [*looking at the photograph*]: Is that him now?

MANDISA: Yes. [*Pause.*] So, what are you going to do on Monday? Are you going back to work again?

SIPHO: Yes.

THANDO: As the Assistant Chief Librarian?

SIPHO: Oh no. To collect my things and my early retirement package of course. They can have the job. I've got other things to do now. I am going to write a letter to President Mbeki. I want to remind him that I voted for him. I put them in power. I paid for this freedom. I paid with my son's life. My brother died in exile. They must never forget the little people like me. The little Assistant Chief somethings who make up the majority that has kept them in power and will still do so for a long time to come. We have dreams too. We have our needs too. Small as they may be they are important to us. We want the 'Better life for all' now! Today! It's our time now.

MANDISA: Bravo!

THANDO: Bravo!

MANDISA: Hey, all this talking has made me very hungry. How about something to eat?

THANDO: I'll make us something to eat quickly. Come Mandisa.

SIPHO: No you two go to town and get us some take aways.

MANDISA: Come with us, Uncle. We all need some air.

SIPHO: No, you two go. I've got things to do.

MANDISA: What now?

SIPHO: Have you both forgotten? We have a funeral tomorrow. We are burying my brother next to my mother's and father's graves.

THANDO *and* MANDISA *prepare to leave*.

SIPHO: You two listen, about Johannesburg, you can both go after the funeral.

THANDO: Daddy I don't know what to say, what to do.

SIPHO: That's the trouble with freedom.

MANDISA: And London?

SIPHO: Don't push your luck. We'll talk about London later, if I am still in a good mood. Mandisa, wait.

He goes into his room and comes back with a photograph of two young boys.

MANDISA: 'Sipho and Themba, 1954.' Thank you!

SIPHO [*embarrassed by her show of affection*]: GO! Thando, don't be long.

[THANDO *and* MANDISA *exit*. SIPHO *picks up the urn*.]

Themba, my brother, I love you. About my wife … it happened.

On Monday I am going to ask my President to give me money to build the first African public library in New Brighton Township for my people. It will be the first in this country. I will move the three small shelves of the African Literature section into the main section of the library. I will be in charge. Mr Sipho Makhaya, Chief Librarian of the African Public Library in New Brighton, Port Elizabeth, South Africa.

He starts to laugh as he imagines himself in the new library.

THE END

Printed and bound by CPI Group (UK) Ltd, Croydon, CR0 4YY

13/04/2025

14656599-0001